Shenandoah Valley Apples

**Frederick County Fruit Growers Association office, Winchester, VA**

*The way to keep land in farming is for farmers to make a profit. It's that simple.*

–Tupper Dorsey

# Shenandoah Valley Apples

Scott Jost

# Contents

Mt. Jackson, Virginia

**Apple Blossom Festival,
Winchester, VA**

National Fruit Product Company
float, Grand Feature Parade.

*Apple Blossom Festival got started in 1924 because all the*
*businesses in town—the hardware store, the grocery store,*
*the equipment store—were in one way or another involved in*
*the apple industry. When the growers had a good year, their*
*employees had a good year, the processors had a good year, the*
*whole town and the whole region had a good year. At that time,*
*there were almost twenty million bushels of apples grown in*
*the state of Virginia. Now it's down to seven and a half million*
*bushels. The number of growers was probably six hundred to a*
*thousand. Now we're probably under a hundred statewide. There*
*were lots of orchards on both sides of the Blue Ridge, and now*
*probably ninety-nine percent of them are inside the Valley.*

–Jim Robinson

# Introduction

by Scott Hamilton Suter

A pair of apple pickers posing with their tools—baskets and a ladder—in Frederick County, Virginia, c. 1910. (Courtesy of Scott Hamilton Suter)

*Shenandoah Valley Apples* presents the history, setting, and values of Virginia's apple-growing region. The voices, both literal and imagistic, succeed, as photographer Scott Jost desires, in raising awareness of "the legacy of one of Virginia's most important and rapidly disappearing cultural landscapes." He details in words and images the cost of sustainable agriculture in an era of chemicals, overland shipping, artificial flavors, and consumer indifference to the sources of their food. Without passing judgment on the actions and fluctuations that have altered this culture, Jost presents stories and images of the land and those who cultivate it. This combination emphasizes that landscapes reflect the values of the humans who steward their surroundings. Confirming Henry David Thoreau's idea that "it is remarkable how closely the history of the apple tree is connected with that of man," the story of apples in the Shenandoah Valley and Blue Ridge regions tells a story of the people of the region, and Jost's photographic journey illustrates a salient portrayal of the twenty-first-century Valley, introducing views of the orchards and voices of the tenders of the land.

Just as the words of growers, packers, and others tell this contemporary tale, voices from the past express the role of the apple in their own eras. As early as the 1720s, cultural observers spoke of the importance of fruit to the welfare and character of individuals and communities in Virginia. William Byrd II, for instance, believed that "those who take care to plant good orchards are, in their general character, industrious people."[1] In those days fruits, including apples, were grown for the use and enjoyment of families and local residents. Without cold storage, fruit was most often turned into liquid, and this affected the cultural consumption of apples. John Joyce, noting his impressions of Virginia in 1785, suggested that "the Drink chiefly used in this Collony [is] generally Cyder, every planter having an orchard, and they make from 1,000 to 5 or 6,000 [gallons],"[2] producing a beverage that ultimately contributed to controversial moral issues regarding the use of alcohol.

Occasionally the apple's conspicuous presence on the landscape named prominent features and localities. Commenting on settler and Native American relations, the Shenandoah Valley's early historian, Samuel Kercheval, identified one such place in 1833: "Tradition relates that several tracts of land were purchased by Quakers from the Indians on Apple Pie Ridge."[3] His casual reference to the ridge reveals that he expected readers' familiarity with the moniker. Similarly, mentioning that spot in an 1854 report of temperature variation in the Valley's slopes and hollows, the renowned Virginia scientist Matthew Fontaine Maury observed, "In Frederick County there is an elevated ridge of land on which apples are so generally safe, when all others in the neighborhood are killed by frosts, that it has acquired the name of Apple Pie Ridge," suggesting that the area had been known by that name for some time.[4]

Maury's important study led to the growth and placement of more orchards in the region, helping introduce the planting of winter apples in the Valley. Speaking to the Virginia State Horticultural Society in 1932, professor Stevenson W. Fletcher declared that "commercial apple culture in Virginia

An apple buyer (right) poses with John Thwaite, grandfather of Diane Kearns, Fruit Hill Orchard near Winchester, Virginia, in the early 1930s. (Courtesy of Diane Kearns)

A roadside vendor offers apples and traditionally crafted items along Highway 250 in the Blue Ridge Mountains near Afton in Nelson County, c. 1940. (Courtesy of Scott Hamilton Suter)

as we know it today began in 1865." He quoted the editor of the agricultural journal *The Farmer*, who wrote in 1866, "Since the War, farmers in the Valley of Virginia have turned their attention to the culture of this fruit, as offering the most speedy and sure means of recuperation to their wasted farms and devastated homes."[5] Of course, apples were an integral part of the Valley diet before they became a commercial product in the second half of the nineteenth century. Soldiers ravishing the region during the War certainly took advantage of this, as Rockingham County resident Michael Shank recalled in 1875. He reminisced, "I had 4 or 5 barrels with vinegar. . . . I reckoned they [Union soldiers] took about 100 gallons." His daughter Fannie, added, "I saw the same troops carry off a large lot of apple butter we had put in crocks in our kitchen loft, over 100 gallons."[6] The efforts of another Valley resident, the farmer and potter Emanuel Suter, support Fletcher's observation regarding the burgeoning commercialization of apples. Suter, eventually the tender of a 7.5-acre orchard featuring more than thirty apple varieties, recorded apple grafting in his diary as early as April of 1866. By the 1890s, Suter was shipping the fruit to brokers in Baltimore and the Midwest. He often noted, for instance, updates such as, "This afternoon I went to the pottery to see about the sale of my apples, a man was here from Zanesville, Ohio wanting to buy." On another occasion he noted that he had "loaded some apples that I sold to John Blosser of Ohio."[7]

Clearly, in the second half of the century, an apple industry began to emerge from the earlier, primarily local, market. Shenandoah Valley farmers, known for their prodigious wheat production prior to and following the Civil War, increasingly planted apple orchards. Historian Kenneth Koons has reported, "The dollar value of orchard production increased nearly fourfold during the period from 1860 to 1880, from nearly 72,000 in 1860 to over 270,000 in 1880."[8] Rail transportation increased market opportunities and growers found buyers in eastern urban centers such as Baltimore, Philadelphia, Washington, D.C., and as far afield as Great Britain. Writing from Albemarle County, Virginia, in 1879, J. F. Wayland commented: "I have been shipping my Pippins direct to Liverpool for the last two seasons. We have, until the last two years, sold direct from the orchard to New York dealers, at $4.00 to $5.00 per barrel."[9] By 1930, apple orchards had nearly replaced wheat fields as the dominant agricultural feature of the Valley's landscape.[10]

In place of the personal recollections of growers and community members, statistics convey the story as the age of the industrial apple emerged. A Virginia orchard survey in 1937 recorded that the Commonwealth's apple growers numbered 3,665, in care of more than four million trees. That year was the peak for Virginia's apple industry as subsequent surveys reflect its gradual decline. By 2005, the number of growers had fallen to 206, with the number of trees totaling 1.5 million. Between 2001 and 2005, the "number of apple trees in Virginia decreased twenty-two percent."[11] Significantly, sixty-nine percent of those trees were in the Shenandoah Valley, indicating a strong local commitment to apple growing.

The commercial apple industry has undeniably contributed in multiple ways to the culture of the Shenandoah Valley. Traditional nineteenth-cen-

Featured in the Virginia Room at the 1939 World's Fair in New York City, this photograph of Shenandoah Valley apple barrels awaiting shipment abroad in Norfolk, Virginia was captioned "the finest of Virginia's apple harvest." (Courtesy of the Library of Virginia)

tury potters turned crocks for apple butter and jugs for cider, vinegar, and brandy. Basket makers fashioned white oak vessels for use by pickers and venders, and coopers produced millions of barrels for shipping apples domestically and abroad. Fortunately, the perceptive work of Scott Jost picks up the story of the apple in the Shenandoah Valley in the industrial era, intertwining sublime images of the landscape with the voices of individuals whose families have lived the stories briefly uttered in this introduction. This book asks us to ponder the significance of the apple to the Valley's heritage, its landscape, and its role in the commerce and culture of the United States, challenging us to contemplate the future of the fruit from our many perspectives and prospects, both culturally and physically.

1. William Byrd II, "History of the Dividing Line betwixt Virginia and North Carolina Run in the Year of Our Lord 1728," in *The Prose Works of William Byrd of Westover*, Ed. Louis B. Wright, (Cambridge: Harvard University Press, 1966), 215.

2. John Joyce, "Virginia in 1785," *The Virginia Magazine of History and Biography*, 23, no. 4 (1915): 410.

3. Samuel Kercheval, A *History of the Valley of Virginia*, 4th ed. (Harrisonburg: C.J. Carrier Company, 1994), 48. Citations refer to the Carrier Edition.

4. Matthew Fontaine Maury, quoted in S.W. Fletcher, "A History of Fruit Growing in Virginia" (reprinted from the Proceedings of the Thirty-Seventh Annual Meeting of the Virginia State Horticultural Society, 1932), 27-28.

5. Fletcher, 27.

6. Emmert F. Bittinger, David Rodes, and Norman Wenger eds., *Unionists and the Civil War Experience in the Shenandoah Valley*, Vol. III (Rockport, ME: Penobscot Press, 2005), 534, 541.

7. Emanuel Suter Diaries, April 13, 1866; November 6, 1893; October 26, 1895, Virginia Mennonite Conference Archives.

8. Kenneth E. Koons, "Wheat in the Regional Farm Economy," in *After the Backcountry : Rural Life in the Great Valley of Virginia*, 1800-1900, ed. Kenneth E. Koons and Warren R. Hofstra (Knoxville: University of Tennessee Press, 2000), 14.

9. Fletcher, 27.

10. Ibid.

11. *Virginia Orchard Survey*, Richmond: USDA/NASS/Virginia Field Office, 2005: 3-5.

Shenandoah Valley Apples

*What does land mean to me? It's fundamental—land. You can stand on your own piece of property and think it's the American dream. It's the American way, owning something. I like hunting and fishing, having a place that you can work with wildlife and hunt and do things. There's privacy. Farming's great; it's very rewarding. It's not necessarily real financially rewarding, but it's very rewarding.*

*Spring comes and it's a renewal, it's a cycle. You can start over. The slate's clean, kind of. You are forever optimistic that this will be a better year. Farmers are very good at that.*

–Tupper Dorsey

## Oakland Orchard, Clarke County, VA

Beehives are placed in the orchard for pollination.

Don't you feel that we've
been surrounded by this all
our lives, that we've lived it?
Our grandparents were doing
it. Our fathers did it. We stayed
in the area and now we have
the opportunity to do it.
—Pem Dorsey Hutchinson

*You plant a tree. You enjoy seeing that tree grow up, and every tree is almost like a child. You work hard to get a good orchard and you pick nice fruit, and I guess it kind of gets into your blood.*

—HENRY CHILES

*It's been a good life. I don't think I would change anything I've done.*

–Robert Solenberger

*I'm a third-generation apple grower. My grandfather started the business in the late 1930s here in Frederick County, and they had a rough time of it in the beginning. I remember stories my father told me about the 1940s when they packed apples in barrels and sent them over to Liverpool, England. My father was seventeen when his dad died, but my father had a brother who was older and they ran the business together. The people in England had to advance money to make the payrolls for our apple company before they even got the apples, and without that help we wouldn't be where we are today. My father and my uncle really built the business up to where it is. We operate a thousand acres now in Virginia and Pennsylvania also. We've always been a fresh-pack oriented company.*

*I went to work for a bank first in Richmond where I learned how to borrow money—which is a handy skill to have—and started in 1979 here in Winchester with both my uncle and my father. The deal was, if I wanted any part of the apple business I had to come back and learn how to sell from my uncle, selling being one of the most important things. My father was the grower; my uncle was the seller. My uncle Fred died three years after I got back, and my father died in 1985. It's never been out of the family.*

–Phil Glaize

*Most every farmer had a little orchard that you would call a family orchard. They planted it so they would have fruit of their own. A lot of farmers had orchards that raised more apples than the family needed, and some people started planting more orchard than they could use. Very few farmers had any containers to put their fruit in, and National Fruit would let you have crates, so they hauled their apples to National Fruit.*

—HENRY BRUMBACK

*In the early days orchards were part of the whole farm, and not just in the case of remnants we find here in Shenandoah National Park, but throughout the colonies. When you acquired land, you didn't really start to improve it until you put an orchard in or planted or built a house. Any of these things were considered proof you were on the land. If you bought property and didn't improve it for a certain number of years, you could lose it. An easy way to improve land was to plant an orchard. You could work later to build your house and outbuildings and everything else. Orcharding has been part of American history from the start.*

—MARA MAISEL

Rockingham County, VA

**Shenandoah National
Park, Madison County, VA**

Apple orchard remnant near
Limberlost trailhead.

Former Freezeland
Orchard Company land,
Warren County, VA

*The orchard has been sold, you know. We sold the whole corporation and they're going to develop it. We had sold some areas along here for lots, but now these people are cutting lots all along. We're right on the ridge. If the Skyline Drive had been extended, this would be Skyline Drive.*

*Here in this Linden area back in the 1900s to about 1940, there were over twenty-two commercial orchards. Now there are none. This is the lowest gap in the Blue Ridge, and this is where the railroad came through first in the early 1800s. The little villages like Linden and Markham all had stations and they had a train. This is where the Shenandoah Valley was discovered. It's beautiful views, and it's in a weather gap. The hillsides drain into the valleys so that you don't get the frost. The orchards started going out right after World War II, and from then on you had the orchard here and the orchard there going out. The Freezeland Orchard was here; the Piedmont Orchard was a ways across the mountain. Charlie Kaiser had orchards all around too.*

–BEN LACY

## Graves Orchard, Syria, VA

*Blossom time is a very picturesque time of year. I was describing to a friend of mine the way the trees are just coming out, how there are miniature leaves on all the trees. This friend used to teach Oriental studies at Columbia University and he said, 'If you like that, then you have the same concept of beauty as the Japanese.' I hadn't really thought about it, that the Japanese say this is the most beautiful time of the year. The buds are just starting to break out, the leaves are just starting to break out, and that's their concept of beauty. I think there's something to that, there really is.*

—PETER COOK

## Tip Top Fruit Farm orchard remnant, Rockingham County, VA

*I remember when I graduated from high school and started to work on the farm. That winter, Father and I worked together. We were going through the orchard cutting out the undesirable limbs, and it just about froze me to death. I kept quiet, but I was miserable. But I have to say for Father, when he was able he was working right with you.*

—Robert Russell

*I'm fifth-generation in the apple industry. My great grandfather came here and started a small commercial kind of operation. It stayed small until my dad entered the picture in 1959, right after he got out of graduate school. Even though he had a degree in chemical engineering, my dad decided he wanted to be a farmer, to basically grow fruit. He took what had been about a hundred acres and has grown it to what we are now, which is almost three thousand acres.*

*Although I'm forty, I'm one of the younger people up-and-coming, which is sad. I mean, that's part of the problem in the apple industry. You can make better money, or a little easier, less risky kind of living, doing something else. As a result, I found myself in these leadership roles where you get involved in things because there are just fewer people. So I'm president of the Frederick County Fruit Growers, and that's our local labor organization, which is providing housing for labor—with a few other services—to members around here. I'm also chair of the Virginia State Apple Board. You get in on it at the state level and it's really interesting to see the whole big picture and watch things change, because literally that's what's happening. The forces that are shaping the industry are just bigger than our regional economy. It'd be nice to keep it like it was, but it's just not gonna happen, so you have to be conscious and realistic and say, Okay, it's an opportunity for change.*

—Diane Kearns

Layman Orchard,
Daleville, VA

## Clarke County, VA

*Once we came out of the Depression and got into World War II—subsequent to World War II—is when the processing industry as we now know it grew. Part of it was because canned food was a convenience for which people were willing to pay, and part of it was because they became too busy. It was economically feasible. Why labor over a kitchen sink? What we're seeing now is an evolution. We went from dried and brined to canned, from canned to frozen and fresh—they overlap. My wife's speculation is that the canned industry has seen its best days, whether it's in vegetables or fruit. It's no longer a convenience item, and people have the money to spend on something that is more tasteful. Frozen lends itself more to microwave preparation.*

There will always be canned food around, but it will not grow. Consequently, since almost all the processors around here are hot packers, they will stop growing. They will cannibalize each other until there are very few left, and once that's established canned will always be there, just like dried fruit. I took dried fruit hiking when I was a kid. I can still buy the same product, but I don't think per capita consumption has changed. More people, but how much dried fruit does one person eat in a lifetime? So it doesn't make any difference how well you manage your business; the industry is changing. Buggy whip manufacturers are out of business.

–BILL HUEHN

## R. R. Ryan and Sons Orchard, Rockingham County, VA

Eric Ryan sprays apples.

*The market situation is not very satisfactory, really. The processors, by and large, try to wait until as late as they can before they come out with their prices. You're faced with a situation in which you are committed. You have made contractual arrangements to send your apples to whatever processor it might be, but until you're well into harvesting that commitment, you don't know what price you're going to get for your crop. Imagine General Motors selling cars and they don't have any idea what price they're going to get for the car until the day they deliver it to the customer.*

—Peter Cook

The processors are having a rough time because it's very competitive on their end and they have to cut cost. The cost, of course, is the fruit. Knowing that they're struggling to have a profit too, I can see that they can't pay much more. But if they can't pay much more, the growers will go out. Which comes first, the processor pulling the plug or the growers pulling the plug? I don't like the way some things are handled in this business, but hey, we're in this business. We can leave, you know. I always say we're stupid. We're sitting around here growing a product and we don't know where we're gonna sell it or how much we're gonna get for it, and investing thousands of dollars.

–TUPPER DORSEY

**Paugh's Orchard,
Shenandoah County, VA**

Harold Paugh picks Red
Delicious apples.

*In 1991, the world grew one billion bushels of apples and the
United States grew two hundred fifty million bushels of apples.
In 2001, the world grew 2.1 billion bushels of apples and the
United States grew two hundred fifty million bushels of apples.
Our competition is fierce, not only from other apples around the
world, but also from other fruit commodities. I was told by one
buyer at Ukrop's Super Market this morning that the movement
of apples in the past two weeks has been very stagnant. I said,
'Is it eastern apples?' and he said, 'It's Washington State also.'*

*'Well Carlton, what is taking the place of that movement?'*

*He says, 'Peaches.'*

*These are all coming from Chile right now. Ten years ago, you
didn't get Chilean grapes, peaches, and nectarines in April; you
bought apples. So the worldwide market has really, really taken
its toll on us, and it's not just the Virginia industry. New York
and Michigan are having the same problems.*

*We're a member of an association that filed an anti-dumping
suit against China for frozen apple juice concentrate. We
were successful. It turns out they were shipping apple juice
concentrate into this country for below production cost. I learned
last night that Mott's, who buys a lot of apples from us, has just
started looking at bringing frozen applesauce in from China.
This would be a new move. You can buy frozen applesauce from
China cheaper than you can buy our apples and make it. We
truly are getting to a point where decisions are going to have to
be made as a country.*

–PHIL GLAIZE

## Fruit Hill Orchard, Winchester, VA

*When I first remember apple picking, we got our pickers from West Virginia. They stayed in the house where my sister lives now. That was my dad's home. They'd put beds upstairs in the house and my mother would feed them. They'd be almost members of the family until we got the apples picked.*

—Henry Brumback

*We had everything from students and faculty from Eastern Mennonite School to German war prisoners who came for a year or so to a temporary camp in the Timberville area. The prisoners were hardly even loosely guarded. I cannot remember who was paid for what.*

—Rowland Shank

Henry Brown, a Jamaican guest worker, with a bin of Golden Delicious apples he picked.

*When I first started running the orchard in the 1950s, we were using 50 percent local help—mountaineer people—and fifty percent people from Greene County who were displaced when Skyline Drive went through. My local people went out completely, so I used all Greene County people. Very soon the Greene County people all started getting Social Security, so I had to go to crews from Mississippi and Alabama. And then very soon welfare and all took the crews away, so I had to start bringing in people from Jamaica through the Frederick County Fruit Growers Association. About that time, the Haitians started coming in, so Jimmy Carter says, 'You gotta take Haitians.'*

*–Ben Lacy*

*The Frederick County Fruit Growers Association charter was formed in 1945. I never quite understood how they got this property, but they bought it from the school board somehow. It's about ten acres that's here in town where the buildings are. Back in the beginning, over a couple of streets on about Smithfield Avenue is where they kept German prisoners, and the German prisoner buildings were wooden sides with tents, like a grain bin. When the war was over and the prisoners all got sent home, they brought those over here for the migrants to live in, and then those were eventually replaced with lean-tos. It says back in the minutes—I don't know, late '40s—where they put doors and windows in the lean-tos. So then the wooden lean-tos by the '50s came to cinder block buildings with individual rooms as is still today. The German prisoners picked the apples and they had different companies in town would hire 'em for so much a day. And one place said you could work German prisoners twelve hours a day and also in the rain. They would note that. I thought that was interesting.*

*They had other people would come before the war—West Virginians and different ones from around—and then men started getting scarce, and that's when the Bahamian program started because there wasn't enough migrants or locals coming to pick 'em. Then that program went so well that they extended it to Jamaicans, and it was about 1978 or 1979 we'd have like seven hundred Jamaicans. As the Jamaican program increased, somehow or other the Bahamians decreased, so they just phased out after about '65, '66, somewhere in there. I'm not sure where.*

*We didn't have Haitians in those days. The first Haitians up here were boat people and they spoke no English and we spoke no Creole, but then, you know, we learned to get along. It was interesting, very interesting. It was probably mid '80s somewhere, I'm thinking, that the crews started to change. We had Haitian crew leaders and it changed from Haitians—we had Haitians and ex-Jamaicans replace the U.S. male, some white and some black, but we very seldom get U.S. males or females in the crews any more. We would have U.S. crew leaders, but we don't any more. They're either ex-Jamaican or Mexican in all cases. We don't have any of the U.S. workers left. I don't know where they went.*

–Carol Burke

Frederick County Fruit
Growers Association labor
camp, Winchester, VA

R. R. Ryan and Sons
Orchard, Rockingham
County, VA

**R. R. Ryan and
Sons Orchard**

Harvesting Gala apples.

My day started around 4:30 this morning. Most of my crew comes in around a quarter to six or six, and I have a little time to try to map out the day. I usually meet with my son around 5:30. We discuss the day's activity, and I primarily do the sales and he does the orchard work. We got another guy that does all the spraying and does all the chemical records, and we have to go through an awful lot now. We try our best to do everything a hundred percent.

When you're selling fruit, you talk to all the customers that you've got and you're always trying to find new ones. You sell a load, then you've got to get it packed and you've got to meet the buyer's specification. Then you've got to get it delivered and trucks are real scarce now because of the way the economy is. I spend a lot of time in the packing house looking at the fruit. I bought a bunch of packing house equipment all over the country—it's new to us but it's used—and it's been about four years putting it all together. We're just making our first runs within the last few days, and still got a lot of things to do.

I heard a professor from Purdue say that anybody wants to survive in agriculture for the next generation has to do things faster, better, and cheaper, and that's what we're trying to do. We might do it faster and we might do it better, but I don't think we're doing it any cheaper. I think that part's not gonna be, so I don't know whether I'm gonna make the grade or not. We will be able to do it better, no doubt about that.

—Henry Chiles

D. K. Russell Orchard
operated by Glaize Apples,
Frederick County, VA

*I ask for crop estimates, and you can tell by the crop estimates about how many workers a person's gonna need. You take three-five—3,500 bushels per worker per season—and use that as a rule of thumb. Some people use three, some people use four.*

–Carol Burke

*We ventured into the wholesale delivery produce business about three years ago. We've got a fair clientele. I pretty much look after all of that, and I drive one of the trucks to do the delivering. My brother looks after most of the farm work. It's been a change for him and me both. I mean, we both did farm work. Now he's got more on him and I've got all this on me, and a lot of my stuff is still in the learning stage. I can get the produce and all bought, but dealing with the customers can take a lot of time. Most of the product has to be exceptionally good because the customers are very, very picky and there's not a lot of money to be made in the wholesale produce business anymore. It's a lot of competition, but it's something diversified. It does give you a cash flow every week, as opposed to waiting five months for a crop to come in. In my opinion, it's a little more positive than raising apples. I know it is. As least you can make something. You've gotta be in line on price, but you sorta set your price on items.*

*This end of the county's growing and you try to consume as much new business as possible. I think there's room in this wholesale business to grow. We've planted some small blocks of fruit, different varieties. I'd say we'll continue to be in the retail business for some time. It just depends on the land value around here. I mean, if somebody came up and offered you a tremendous amount of money for this piece of property here, you could hardly turn it down.*

—Mark Ikenberry

*From what I've read, in Botetourt County alone back in the 1940s and 1950s and maybe into the early 1960s there were over a thousand acres of orchard. Some were small, but they had a few large growers. I don't know if it's even five hundred acres now. My family's was always a commercial operation until we started doing some retail business in 1976. We had a crop failure and just had about six thousand bushels of apples. We had to have something to do with them, so we started in the retail business and have continued that up to now.*

*The southern part of Virginia is more of a fresh apple region— although we still have some processing apples—probably because of the freight and the distance to Winchester. In this area you've got fairly decent elevations. It is rolling hills with some high ground and some low ground too, but pretty suitable for most varieties. We used to sell apples to Kroger, A&P, and places like that. Local stores bought local apples, not like it is now.*

–Mark Ikenberry

*As late as 1985 there were thirty-three applesauce producers in the U.S., and as late as last year there were only twelve of 'em going into the retail trade. We're basically all retail-oriented— the Walmarts, Safeways, Wynn-Dixies, A&Ps, Krogers, etcetera. We sell to all the major chains. We're almost a hundred percent private label. We sell under everyone else's label, and we treat it as if it's our own. We've been pretty successful staying in the business. We ship apple juice all over the United States. We ship applesauce as far west as Denver. We are currently the sixth largest apple grower in the United States. We have about four thousand acres of land which we call orchards. I think we have almost three thousand acres of planted orchard.*

–Sonny Bowman

**Ikenberry Orchard,
Botetourt County, VA**

Apple and peach orchards.

### Ikenberry Orchard

A tractor prepares soil
for sweet corn.

*We have a small family orchard, just twelve hundred trees on eight acres. I was gonna do early retirement from my other job and then slide into this, and it worked out real well. By the time I retired, the production was going pretty decent to keep my income level up.*

*I originally intended to sell to the processing plants. The price was high at that time, but by the time I got in the market and went to sell, they weren't paying anything. I had a bunch of apples and they did too, and I realized this wasn't gonna work. So I just went out in front and started selling what I could off the back of my pickup truck. I sold off that on Saturday and Sunday, and then we built a shed on a farm wagon and sold off that. Then we built this shed. It got better every year somewhat. We originally had about two thousand trees on twenty acres. So we rearranged the orchard and downsized it and got into more varieties.*

*We have peaches too. I also raise pumpkins and sweet corn, and I'm having an awful time with the sweet corn but it complements the market and gives it more variety for the customer. You have to have a seasonal look, and gourds and Indian corn decorations turned out real well with me.*

–Robert Mowery

Ryan's Farm Market,
Rockingham County, VA

Mowery Orchard Farm
Market, Woodstock, VA

## George's Garden Place, Rockingham County, VA

Pressing cider.

*One of the ways we could really introduce apples with flavor to our citizens is through the schools. The lunch programs. For goodness sakes take that Red Delicious out; put in a Pippin or a Grimes Golden and see how the kids react to it. And all you have to do—it's kind of like that garbology thing—is study the garbage and how many ate down to the core.*

—Tom Burford

*In 1939 my grandfather and my father and my father's brother came to a sale here where the plant is located today. My grandfather paid three thousand dollars for a cheese factory that had been converted to make applesauce, and the first year that we ran it I think we made twelve hundred cases of applesauce the entire fall. Of course fresh apples were a staple back in the 1930s, but you couldn't sell the low-grade to the consumers and the export was only on the medium grades up. He bought the applesauce plant so that he would have a home for all his second-grade apples. Back in the formative days, you would start packing traditionally the day after Labor Day and you would always be finished by Thanksgiving.*

—SONNY BOWMAN

*Winchester Cold Storage built their first cold storage in 1917, and it was probably four hundred thousand bushels. In 1920, they built the next one, and it was probably six hundred thousand bushels. Then in 1929, they built a third building that took them to about a million and a half. It was the boom in apples. In the early years before cold storage, you packed immediately and sold for whatever the price was. But with cold storage, you could store apples and the price would go up after harvest. You could afford to pay the cold storage fees because the apples became more valuable.*

*The English, during World War 2 or right before, started experimenting with low-oxygen storage, and by the early 1950s had a commercially viable thing going. With controlled atmosphere storage, you could keep apples you picked in September and ship them out next September, and that is what really allowed Washington State to dominate the apple business. I think it was in the early 1980s that Washington State finally had enough controlled atmosphere and enough crop to market year-round. Virginia had trouble growing an extra-fancy Red Delicious, which was the heart of the crop. Extra-fancy has to be ninety percent red, essentially. Virginia grew one grade down—fancy, or an extra fancy/fancy combination. But as long as Washington State can deliver the extra-fancy brand year-round, you don't sell to the big marketing chains when they can get the same quality from one source.*

—TOM MACCUBBIN

50

Winchester Cold Storage,
Winchester, VA

Apple sculpture,
Winchester, VA

*We had this thing called the Liars Club, and basically it was all these growers from Maryland, West Virginia, Virginia, and Pennsylvania. We'd meet in Winchester and discuss what the prices were in our various packing houses and how we were doing. Nobody ever told the truth, you know, because we didn't want anybody to figure it out. But we still got together, and some pretty good information came out of the meetings.*

*I remember when all the old guard was going off and all the sons were coming on, and they were trying to maintain what their fathers had done. I remember sitting there one day with them and I said, You guys, you must understand one thing. Times are changing and we are not our fathers. We've got to change with the times. That's probably one of the few things I got to contribute to this group, but that's where I got my two cents in. Even though we wanted to be as successful, we were not our fathers. And things were changing, sometimes faster than we wanted them to.*

–Jim Robinson

*Appearance doesn't make a lot of difference for the processing apples and it does for the fresh market. Spraying, thinning—it's a pretty involved process. We work on the trees every day of the year. It's something that takes a lot of nursing care. You don't just plant and forget about them. To grow fresh apples, we have to do more pruning and probably more detail pruning and opening up the limbs so you get light in, and hand thinning. You have to separate the apples out individually on the rim rather than let them be in a cluster if you want to get full color.*

–HENRY CHILES

*The consumer goes into the market and says, We need fresh apples, puts a bag of Red Delicious in the cart, takes it home. They dump the bag into the fruit bowl then take the one off the top, bite into it: This isn't very good. It would go in the garbage. Then they were put into children's lunchboxes and the children would either have an apple battle with them or throw them out. The rest would rot in the bowl. They'd dump 'em in the garbage. The next week they'd get their cart and push it and say, We need apples. They would ritually go through this fifty-two weeks of the year, and you can imagine if you took fifty-two bags of Red Delicious and piled 'em up how much compost you're getting.*

–TOM BURFORD

**Madison County, VA**

Apples rejected by the processor.

**Former Tip Top Fruit Farm orchard, Rockingham County, VA**

Falling blossoms overlay last year's apples.

*I did an apple tasting at the arboretum. They had set this thing up, and there were a lot of diplomats arriving and their limousines were pulling in. This one woman came in. It was cold. She had furs and was dripping in diamonds sort of thing. After the tasting we had all the apples in baskets lined up, and people would come up and ask questions. So this woman dripping in diamonds came up and she was standing in front of this Calville Blanc which is the classic dessert apple of France. She sort of looked around like this and this, reached over, and got one and stuck it in her pocket. Stole that apple. Apparently she was really impressed. Probably the only thing she's ever had to steal in her life.*

–TOM BURFORD

*When you're picking a bushel of apples, you hope that ninety percent of 'em are perfect apples where you can pack and ship, but it's not gonna always be that way. You got a bruise on it or something, that apple's got to go to the processors and the processors are getting pickier than they used to be. Everything's gotta pretty much be perfect for them too because of the way the peelers work. You can't have any hail hit 'em and you can't get too big and you can't get too small. That three-inch apple's the ideal apple they want.*

–JAMES GRAVES

*It's the American way. You want it big, red, and shiny.*

–TUPPER DORSEY

**Former Burkholder orchard,
Rockingham County, VA**

Apple trees are removed to create
pasture for grazing cattle.

*If you had a young orchard and you wanted to sell that piece of land, it'd be a liability. Who wants to buy land with an apple orchard on it and lose two, three dollars a bushel raising apples? Basically, what an apple orchard is worth is whatever the stripped land is worth less what it costs to push out the trees.*

*We were down to another grower's the other night, and he had a fifty-acre plot there and he showed us the figures on what it cost him to plant it. He had about four thousand dollars an acre just in planting costs. He'd put irrigation in it, so knock it back to three thousand dollars an acre to plant trees. Three thousand dollars an acre for the land, that's six thousand dollars right there. Then you put another minimum five hundred dollars an acre a year in it for five years to get the orchard into production, and you're looking at seven, eight, nine thousand in total. When you go to sell an orchard, you fill out a financial statement and it's worth about two thousand dollars an acre. It's worth three thousand less a thousand to clean the damn thing up. So then you're down almost five thousand dollars an acre.*

*If you sell an orchard, you'd probably sell it to someone in northern Virginia who wanted to be a gentleman farmer or a retired something. I don't think anyone would want it for an apple orchard right now.*

—CARROLL RYAN

R. R. Ryan and Sons
orchard, Rockingham
County, VA

It used to be you had a one-on-one with the buyer—your broker did—and you could call them up and say Scott, I got this size fruit. You think you could use it? Oh yeah, and send me two loads or whatever. Now it is Scott who? I don't know who you are.

—BILL FLIPPIN

When you can ride to Arlington and get twenty dollars an hour, it's kind of hard to get anybody to work on the farm for seven or eight dollars an hour.

—HENRY BRUMBACK

*Even the retail business was better years ago. We didn't have any competition here much. Kroger's two miles down the road from us now. When they all move in that hurts because the consumer's gonna go there, and just like going to Walmart they stop one time and get it all and go home. You got husband and wife both working, you know, their time makes a lot of difference.*

—MARK IKENBERRY

*Our forefathers had foresight enough to give us a structure that permits us to optimize our activities, and we don't even appreciate it. We have the opportunity to succeed, and we have the opportunity to fail. Even failure indicates to somebody else what does not work. It's natural. If someone goes bankrupt because they didn't have the right idea someone else is watching and will say, That was the wrong idea. The government didn't say, Don't worry, I'll prop you up. Our structure is the basic determinant. But our farmers still have to compete against other people. The growers will change form; they'll adapt. Incrementally, they'll make a lot of small changes. They'll have to; they will. What all of those changes are, I have no idea. More sons and daughters will leave the farm; larger farms will be run by fewer and fewer people. The shake-out will mean that only those with a natural advantage and those with the right marketing strategy will form part of a successful matrix. Maybe someone will grow herbs and flowers and ornamentals—and some apples.*

–Bill Huehn

*I think in the end, you're going to wind up with the really big people that are growing for a processor, and you're going to wind up with the little people that have a market and they're selling some kind of specialty something. And then there are people like us who are caught in the middle.*

–Carol Swanson

Oakland Orchard,
Clarke County, VA

Fruit Hill Orchard,
Winchester, VA

*Western fruit, in my not-so-unbiased opinion, is terrible stuff that is bred for looks and shipping but not for taste quality. It is a terrible affront to the eastern United States. I used to throw better apples than that at fence posts for target practice.*

–ROWLAND SHANK


*By and large, Washington State's apples look better than ours do, so they're getting the lion's share of the business right now— however, at cheap prices. If the grocery stores don't get apples cheap enough, they'll put Chilean nectarines on the shelf. As far as the chain stores are concerned, it's all a matter of shelf space and how many dollars they can turn on that shelf space.*

–PHIL GLAIZE

## Former Tip Top Fruit Farm orchard, Rockingham County, VA

Picnic table placed among abandoned apple trees by the current property owner.

*I'm involved in the U.S. Apple Association which primarily represents all of the states, and I'm involved in the U.S. Apple Export Committee which is seven states joined together and we basically go head-to-head with Washington State. I guess we've done some good. We've made some inroads in some new markets. Our position's been that every year you've got to be looking for new markets because things change so fast. You get a good market and maybe it'll be good for a couple of years. Then something will happen and so you've gotta be four or five years ahead looking down the road and be in a position when opportunity comes.*

—Henry Chiles

There are plenty of people to eat all the apples that we could ever grow, soon as we get smart enough to figure out how to market all our apples in Virginia. Seems to me there might be more emphasis being put on local produce—on buying Virginia apples. I guess they've done several surveys and people may buy more according to price than where they come from. I think of Virginia apples and Washington State apples, they're probably going to buy which one looks the best rather than where it comes from. There are plenty of people here, no question about that. If I'm not mistaken, I think seventy percent of the people in the United States are within 500 miles of Charlottesville or Richmond or something like that.

—HENRY CHILES

**Harrisonburg, VA**

Apple tree viewed from the
author's back yard.

## Showalter Orchard, Augusta County, VA

*I do not know of another orchard in Augusta County. If you would get off at Mint Spring and go to Route 11, go back toward Staunton, and then turn to your left, there was a big orchard in there at one time, Mr. John Neff, and he had his own packing shed and all that. I remember just close by there, Russell Shank, he had a big orchard and that's all out. Lyle Kendig was from here toward Stuarts Draft just several miles. Big Orchard. That's no more.*

*I think what happened for a lot of these fellows, as they retired there was no one there really to take over, and I'm sure that's true here too. We have three sons but they're involved in other work and I can understand that. J Hannon Morris was one of the last orchards to go out that I can remember. That's down here on 250. They have the packing shed and they still sell produce there, probably apples, but I'm sure they're brought in from across the mountain or from some other location. Mr. Loving had orchards around. Jack Young, Simmons Brothers. There were just a whole lot of different orchards around, and they're gone.*

—RICHARD SHOWALTER

## Graves Orchard, Syria, VA

Abandoned sprayer.

*We had a Walmart go in across the street, and then another commercial outfit next to me too. There are plans to build a golf course behind me. So yes, the landscape's starting to change. We're zoned R-2, and that means multiple density housing. If someone around me starts selling, then it'll just domino, see? Right now I haven't got anybody around me that I'm concerned about, but if housing would come right up against me, then I would be concerned about spraying.*

*Ten years from now there will probably be multiple density housing or some commercial something on my land. There is growth here in the county, and it's moving this way. The way things are going, it's just moving right on, you know? And the apple people are disappearing. Every dog has its day, and the apple industry here has just about had its day.*

—ROBERT MOWERY

Ikenberry Orchard,
Botetourt County, VA

*We've only been farming just over two hundred acres of apples now, whereas twenty years ago we probably had twelve to fourteen hundred acres. I enjoyed apples, but I must say that over the period I've been here—twenty-four years—so much of it was a struggle. We're dealing with debt, financing, the banks, and so much of your focus was on that and not the actual growing of fruit. And it was not profitable, so I didn't get a real thrill out of it. In the nursery business we're into now it's, How do you do it right? That's a much nicer way to go about your business than, How can I keep cutting costs? Do I miss it? No, not really. But had it been profitable, I'd be answering you completely differently.*

—Tupper Dorsey


*You've got to come up with other ideas of how to use apples and things. Right now we've only got about ten or twelve acres of pick-your-own and we're putting in another ten or twelve more acres. The reason we're expanding is for the school kids. We have a beehive inside of a building in glass so you can see the bees working. Then we take the kids out and show 'em how the bees pollinate the apples. We have what we call the farm tour. We've got aquatic life that we do. Whatever the schools want we will try to take care of 'em. We like to run somewhere between a hundred and two hundred kids a day. They want to come out and pick an apple or come out and pick a pumpkin, so we take a hayride and do that. Then we got into Standards of Learning. We've got people qualified to teach that. We have chickens and we have pigs and you try to have baby pigs born and do the eggs. We have a cloned steer up there that we got from a research station and we've got llamas. We've got goats; we've got sheep, rabbits, and all kinds of things so the kids can see 'em.*

—James Graves

## Madison County, VA

Orchard downsizing.

*I've had a good life with what*
*I've done. I don't have my heart*
*in the apple industry like I used*
*to. It used to be that it was my*
*interest; it's waning now. I think*
*it's age and economics. I can see*
*it's really labor intensive, and*
*it's a labor of love. I guess I've*
*lost that love. I want to see my*
*employees benefit from it, and they*
*can't get anything out of it but*
*money because they're punching*
*the clock. When you've got a guy*
*that's worth twenty dollars an*
*hour and you can only pay him*
*twelve, you know that guy could*
*do better for himself if he moved*
*on. We've lost the shoe industry.*
*We've lost the steel industry.*
*We've lost half the automobile*
*industry, and the textiles are gone*
*basically. And, you know, we may*
*not be able to raise our fruit as*
*cheap as other countries anymore*
*and that's maybe the real world.*

—Bill Flippin

**Rockingham County, VA**

Apple trees transplanted from
the former Burkholder orchard
to alongside a rural driveway.

**Former Burkholder
orchard, Rockingham
County, VA**

Ash pile from burned
apple trees.

## Woodstock, VA

Orchard being pushed out for development.

*Our 401-K is in this land. We don't have a bank account, not anything much, and yet when farmers want to develop because they need the money to retire on, the governments throw things at you. You can't do this; you can't do that. We don't know whether we'll let you develop or not. These people who've gone to Arlington and gotten a job—or even Winchester—they already have their retirement where they can put their finger on it right now, and they never give us any consideration. They want to keep all of your land in open space so they can enjoy it.*

—GLADYS BRUMBACK

84

*We may become as dependent upon other people to provide our foodstuffs as the Brits and the Japanese. We're going to fuss and scream, but it's parallel with our dependency on oil. Oil and food. The capitalist system says, He who does something best should enjoy the business. If someone else owns the oil, and someone else owns the food-producing capacity, we will become dependent upon the caprice of someone else. We will have sold some of our independence.*

–Bill Huehn

*At first it was pretty much held as a sacred tenet that apples are either red or yellow, and we had the two big ones to prove it. Then that was blown out of the water by Mrs. Granny Smith. Then came along these striped ones and blushed ones. Of course the Gala could not make its mind up. And the Fuji. There was an orchardist on the west coast who said, I'll give anyone ten thousand dollars to bring me as red a strain of Fuji as you can find. So the old stereotype is still working.*

*However, there are those including myself who have retrieved many varieties out of the past that are alien to what apples are thought of as being. Along comes the russet apple, this brown apple that looks like a potato skin. And in markets like Dupont Circle in Washington or the green market in Union Square in New York, and in tastings that are being done—a lot of historic sites that I am involved with are doing them—the people are discovering. And it's a remark I often get after a tasting: I did not realize that apples could have so many tastes. People are beginning to find their taste preferences. There are people who like sweet apples; people who like very tart apples. But people are eating and discovering. Oh yeah, these are real tart apples. I like these. I'll buy these. And every taster is a walking billboard for don't eat those supermarket apples. Go look around. Find a little shop. Go to your farmers market. You'll find somebody in there selling a few.*

–Tom Burford

*Back in the '80s, Red Delicious was a good variety. But where you used to pack a seventy five percent to full color extra fancy, now you've got to have it ninety-five to full. It's hard for us to get that kind of color, so you're back to a lesser grade of apple and it's less money for you. You plant twenty, thirty, forty acres of orchard and just because it doesn't color up you don't go in there and push 'em out, because it's no way to get your investment back. So you have to sort of live with it and do the best you can. Some varieties are almost obsolete now. Law Rome was a good variety in the '80s. Did real well with 'em for a while, and then all of a sudden the processor won't use 'em because the meat gets streaked red and it changes the color of their sauce. Jonathan's another variety that's basically not used anymore. Some of these newer varieties like Gala have taken the place of these other apples, and they're a whole lot better apple. You go to the apple meetings and here's a guy that says, Well these Galas, that's gonna be the next big thing. You need to be planting those. But you think in the back of your mind, well, you've been selling these older varieties for fifty years. Is this new one gonna take off that good? And maybe you didn't plant as many or plant 'em in time. That was a big factor because at one time those new things brought in real good money. Now everybody starts planting 'em so the price drops.*

—Mark Ikenberry

*My father used to say an apple grower is the stubbornist human being in the world. They would rather go to hell by themselves than heaven with their apple-growing neighbor. And they are. All of us are stubborn. All of us are opinionated, and soon there won't be many of us.*

—Sonny Bowman

We put quite a bit of emphasis into visiting buyers, and we try to get the overseas buyers to come here. If you can get someone to come in and they like what they see, you got a better chance of selling to them. We broke into the Mexican market two years ago for the first time. So far that looks like it's gonna help us, and Mexico is a pretty fast-growing country. Their economy is getting better and we see that as a potential market for the next few years. It's super-complicated shipping in there because of the restrictions they put on us. They have to have their inspectors up here and see the apples sealed up in a room. The apples have to be sealed up for ninety days and then they have to come back and stand here and watch you pack 'em. Plus we have to foot the bill for all that. Probably our government's doing the same thing to them for other products.

We were lucky enough to get some federal grant money that promotes exports and helps bear some of that expense. All forty-eight states got some proportion of the money. It had to be used for the promotion of exports, and we've been very lucky that several things like that have really helped us to expand the export markets. We compete against pretty much all the major apple-producing states. New York, Pennsylvania, Michigan, we all worked together but I guess generally whoever's got the low price gets the order. It's pretty competitive, and I guess our expenses have gone up quite a bit in the last few years and the price of apples hasn't gone up that much. We think we're selling a good product and we remain hopeful that there will be a market for good apples—somewhere.

–Henry Chiles

Alson H. Smith, Jr.
Agricultural Research
and Extension Center,
Frederick County, VA

*I remember going to a meeting one time when the growers were talking about boycotting one of the processors, and it was a secret meeting because they didn't want the processors to be there. We were meeting at night in a secluded place to try to discuss issues of how to get apple prices up without being identified or targeted by the different processors, and these guys were getting so passionate because it was their livelihood. But not only that. They loved it, you know? The last thing these guys wanted to do was to have to sell their farms. They wanted to stick with it. Raising apples was an art. Pruning trees was an art. Selling apples was an art. Some of these guys—some of these men and women, I should say—were so good at it.*

–Jim Robinson

*You really have to struggle with your imagination to think how fertile the earth was and how friable, when people could actually run a hand down into soil and pull up and lift it like this. And you could think too, that every apple you ate and tossed the core away, the earth would sort of embrace it and those seeds would germinate. It was so fecund. Everything was just in a state of great fertility. Our concept of soil today is dirt. It's something ugly, dead. Don't get it on you; don't bring your dirt in the house. And not realizing how it's part of the lifeline, that there should be this sharp communication between the person and that dirt. But I think that's gonna really figure prominently in what happens, being more aware of it and not building a subdivision on it or building— goodness knows—these supermarkets, these malls.*

–Tom Burford

**Fruit Hill Orchard, Winchester, VA**

Mature apple trees that will soon be pushed out and replanted to increase productivity.

I've got two sons that are here.
They've got five children—three
boys and two girls—and they're
around here all the time. I would
be generation number five on
this farm right here, but I'm the
number twelve generation since
we got started. I've got thirteen—
my son—and his son is fourteen.

–JAMES GRAVES

*We're diversified enough.
We're lean and mean. I think
we can survive as well as
anybody, but it's tough. I want
the land to stay in the family.*
—Robert Solenberger

## Berryville, VA

Orchard remnants surround Berryville Printing.

*A friend of mine, he had land right here near Berryville. And some guy came in and offered him—now this was back about 1990—ten thousand dollars an acre for, like, two hundred acres of orchard and gave him a lease for ten years for a dollar a year. He said, 'What would you have done?' I said I'd have made sure that gentleman got home to get to his checkbook safely.*

—SONNY BOWMAN

**Freezeland
Orchard Company,
Warren County, VA**

Farmstead being sold for
development.

**Silver Creek Orchard,
Nelson County, VA**

*One of the most impressive things I can remember was a man and his son down in Nelson County. The man was eighty-three years old, and he ordered in enough apple trees to plant twenty acres. I said to him, 'You're never gonna see the apples off of those trees.' And he said, 'No but there were apple trees when I came here, so there are gonna be trees when I leave.' That impressed me a whole lot, that they weren't just selfish. They were looking ahead. They were stewards of the land.*

–R.L. HORSBURGH

I call myself a realist but my brothers and sisters call
me a pessimist. I'm saying it will never work; we're not
gonna make a living. But I've stayed here for almost
forty years and we've made a living. I guess if you count
my grandfather and then my mother and myself, I'd be
the third generation.

—BILL FLIPPIN

## Silver Creek Orchard, Nelson County, VA

Young dwarf apple trees.

*I used to know a guy, and he just loved pruning trees. He said that every tree to him was a piece of art. He worked for D. K. Russell, and he couldn't have worked for a finer family. They were the artists in our region of the apple industry. You went to their orchards and everything was perfect. Their apples were spaced up on the trees, you know? It was like walking into a picture.*

—Jim Robinson

*I'm fifty-five years old. I'm English. I married an American and we lived in London for several years then moved here to Virginia in 1977. We bought a house and a piece of property in Clarke County, and no sooner had we done that than a piece of property came up for sale right in our viewshed. That property was an apple orchard, and we ended up buying it partly because it seemed like a good investment and secondly to stop anybody else from getting it and building houses. There was even talk of building a factory there. I'm interested in history and preservation, so I got into it that way.*

*For the first three years I employed a manager to run the orchard. Although I knew a certain amount about farming from when I was a teenager, I didn't know everything about apples. I learned under this man for three years, and since about 1980 I've been running it myself.*

*The orchard was planted in 1955 by the Byrd family— Senator Byrd—whose family comes from here in Clarke County. The Byrds had apple orchards up and down this highway, US 340, partly because the land was good. And I suspect Senator Byrd also had an eye on real estate being accessible to the main highway and fairly close to Washington. He was smart enough to know that this would be a smart long-term real estate investment.*

–Peter Cook

## Oakland Orchard,
## Clarke County, VA

Peter Cook, Oakland Orchard
owner, and Percy Williams,
Frederick County Fruit Growers
Association camp manager.
Peter Cook is a first-generation
apple grower. Percy Williams
has been camp manager for
more than fifty years.

Clarke County, VA

# Oral Histories

Gordon D. "Sonny" Bowman II is President, Bowman Apple Products Company, Inc., Mt. Jackson, Virginia. He is a third generation in the apple industry.

Gladys B. Brumback is Bookkeeper, Woodbine Farms, Inc., Frederick County, Virginia.

Henry M. Brumback is Partner and former President, Woodbine Farms, Inc., Frederick County, Virginia. He is a third generation apple grower.

Tom Burford is an orchard and nursery consultant, author and apple historian from Monroe, Virginia.

Carol Burke is General Manager, Frederick County Fruit Growers Association, Winchester, Virginia.

Henry Chiles, Owner of Graves Mountain Lodge, Batesville, Virginia, is a third generation apple grower.

Peter J. Cook is Partner, Oakland Orchard, Clarke County, Virginia, and President, Old Time Apple Growers Association, Winchester, Virginia. He is a first generation apple grower.

Tupper H. Dorsey is President, Moore and Dorsey Inc., Berryville, Virginia. He is third generation in the apple industry.

Bill Flippin is a third generation apple grower from Tyro, Virginia.

Phil Glaize is Owner, Glaize Apples, Winchester, Virginia. He is third generation in the apple industry.

James Graves is Owner of Graves Mountain Lodge. He is a second generation apple grower. His family has been farming in Virginia for 14 generations.

Robert L. Horsburgh, Stephens City, Virginia, is Emeritus Professor of Entomology and retired Director, Alson H. Smith Agricultural Research and Extension Center, Winchester, Virginia.

William G. Huehn is retired Shenandoah Valley Apple Buyer for National Fruit Product Company, Winchester, Virginia.

Pembroke D. Hutchinson is Secretary, Moore and Dorsey, Inc., Berryville, Virginia. Her family has been in the apple business three generations.

**Mark Ikenberry** is Partner, Ikenberry Orchard, Dalesville, Virginia. He is fourth generation in the apple industry.

**Diane Kearns** is Treasurer, Fruit Hill Orchard, Winchester, Virginia and President, Frederick County Fruit Growers Association. She is fifth generation in the apple industry.

**Ben R. Lacy III** is President, Linden Beverage Company, Linden, Virginia, and formerly President and Manager, Freezeland Orchard Company, Linden, Virginia. His family has been in the apple industry since 1906.

**Tom Maccubbin** is Eastern Operations Manager, Poly Processing Company, Winchester, Virginia, and formerly Manager, Winchester Cold Storage, Winchester, Virginia.

**Mara Meisel** is Naturalist, Shenandoah National Park, Luray, Virginia.

**Robert S. Mowery** is Owner, Mowery Orchard-Farm Market, Woodstock, Virginia. He is a first generation apple grower.

**James R. Robinson** is Assistant Manager, Linden Beverage Company, Linden, Virginia, and Secretary-Treasurer and Vice President, R & T Packing Company, Winchester, Virginia. His family has been in the apple business four generations.

**J. Robert Russell** is Secretary and formerly President, D. K. Russell and Sons, Inc., Clearbrook, Virginia. His family has been in the apple business four generations.

**Carroll R. Ryan** is Partner, Ryan's Orchard and Fruit Market, Timberville, Virginia. His family has been in the apple business three generations. The farm has been in his family eight generations.

**Rowland Shank** is a retired clinical psychologist. Mr. Shank was third generation in his family's orchard business, J. Ward Shank, which operated near Broadway, Virginia until 1952.

**C. Robert Solenberger** is President, Fruit Hill Orchard, Winchester, Virginia. He is a fourth generation apple grower.

**Richard Showalter** is a second-generation apple grower from Waynesboro, Virginia.

**Carol B. Swanson**, Woodbine Farms, Inc., Frederick County, Virginia. Her family has grown apples for four generations.

# Epilogue

*by* Scott Jost

I never liked apples that much when I was growing up. The apples my mother purchased from the grocery store in our small South-Central Kansas town came from Washington State. You know the ones: large, deep red, waxy skin, sort of flavorless, uniform. Apples were apples.

While the food I ate wasn't very interesting and most of it—even bread—seemed to come from somewhere else, I did acquire an appreciation for the infinite variations of light, color, and contour at play in the local landscape. In college, my art professor and mentor, Robert Regier, helped me formalize in my paintings and prints a way of seeing and representing those patterns and relationships unique to the natural and agricultural landscapes in Kansas.

Several years later, I was driving from my parents' home in Newton back to grad school in Minneapolis. That morning great clouds of topsoil soared overhead in a gusty, dissonant south wind blowing in the beautiful Kansas light. Those colors, shapes, and patterns so enjoyable to paint were quickly being erased by forces beyond my control and more significantly, I realized, beyond the control of wheat farmers whose land was being carried away forever. That experience and others like it helped me form a commitment to land stewardship, an appreciation for the importance of agriculture and agrarian traditions and a sense of participation in the land's productive bounty that informs this work.

In 1996, my wife Kathy and I relocated to the central Shenandoah Valley of Virginia. At the Harrisonburg Farmer's Market, we bought apples from George Merz, a local grower who raised thirty-two apple varieties on just over 3 acres and pressed an exceptionally sweet cider. George's apples came in all sizes, shapes, colors, textures, and flavors. Some of his varieties

were heirlooms; others were relatively new. Very few resembled the iconic western Red Delicious of my youth. These were apples!

By discovering and tasting local apples, I began to realize that apples are—or have been—just about everywhere in Virginia. While George's compact orchard thrived to the west of Harrisonburg, the Tip Top Fruit Farm's vine-covered remnants languished between new suburban homes just east of town. Blocks of well-tended commercial orchard are still visible from Interstate 81 in Shenandoah County, and farther north Mt. Jackson's water tower is a huge, shiny trompe loeil basket of red apples. At Woodstock, a Walmart, a Ford dealership, and two-story apartment complexes gradually replace rows of apple trees where tent caterpillars are as thick as the apples once were. Each site is a reminder that apples represent an important cultural landscape legacy in Virginia. Virginia's apple culture is as deep-seated and proud as the wheat culture I grew up around in Kansas. When I think about Virginia now, I think about apples.

Many photographs and interviews in *Shenandoah Valley Apples* were made in Winchester and Frederick County, where Virginia's apple industry is still most active and visible. Others were made in Albermarle, Augusta, Botetourt, Clarke, Madison, Nelson, Rockingham, Shenandoah, and Warren counties in the Shenandoah Valley and Blue Ridge regions of Virginia. Perspectives include those of first- through fifth-generation apple growers as well as representatives of industry groups, associations, and related businesses, a variety of apple industry workers, and self-described apple historians. Orchards range from a 9-acre roadside operation through mid-sized orchards on diversified family farms, to some of the nation's largest commercial orchards. Photography subjects were chosen to exemplify important aspects of apple growing in Virginia. Interview participants were chosen for their involvement in, knowledge of, and concern for apple growing in Virginia. Interviews and photographs do not attempt a comprehensive documentation of Virginia apples. Rather, in approaching the fieldwork, I photographed and interviewed until convinced I had reached an understanding of the people, land, and issues involved that could be shared with others.

Through my fieldwork, I came to understand that Virginia apples represent a cultural legend exemplified by relationships between people and land in the context of an economy that has always been regional, national, and international in nature. *Shenandoah Valley Apples* also describes a unique present in which dissonant winds in this economy are changing those people and that land with unprecedented severity and speed. Though Virginia is the nation's sixth-largest apple producer, economic pressures, international trade, and encroaching development are changing the industry and its people dramatically. Between 1977 and 2005, apple acreage in Virginia decreased by more than half and sixty-five percent of all growers left the business. When I think about apples now, I realize that Virginia is increasingly without them—and without apple growers. At the same time, stories of adaptation, perseverance, and success are also part of the picture.

This book primarily embodies the perspective of apple growers—those who own the land they farm. To a great extent, land ownership determines land-use and stewardship practices. Yet changes in the economy and society change the people who own that land, in turn affecting the land and its health. A project of this nature, therefore, represents an interpretive act.

While I personally favor efforts to preserve family farms, agricultural land, and a healthy ecology, this project does not attempt to raise issues such as the drawbacks versus merits of chemical spraying. In weaving together these stories, I wish to honor the integrity of those stories as told to me.

I hope *Shenandoah Valley Apples* will help preserve the legacy of one of Virginia's most important and rapidly disappearing cultural landscapes, raise awareness of and concern for apple growing in Virginia, and in the process draw our attention toward broader social, economic, and environmental change issues affecting agriculture and land use everywhere that are exemplified by apple growing. I wish to affirm experiences with and efforts on behalf of apple growing for people who participated in the project, and recognize the wisdom, insights, and examples these people may offer to others.

I experienced a certain amount of dissonance and guilt while working on this project. That sense of physical beauty I developed as a young painter involving light, color, pattern, and texture would overwhelm my senses when photographing in an orchard heavy with fruit, sometimes only a few minutes after its owner told me he might be better off from an economic standpoint letting that fruit hit the ground. This conflict between an appreciation for intact and working rural and agricultural landscapes, on the one hand, and our inability or unwillingness to figure out how to keep local farmers economically viable, on the other, is something those of us who don't farm must come to terms with. At the very least, I agree with Tom Burford: "We should be ashamed of ourselves as Virginians that we eat apples coming from another place, because there is no other state in the country that has as rich an apple heritage as we have."

# Author Biographies

**Scott Jost**, Associate Professor of Art, lives in Harrisonburg, Virginia and teaches photography and design at Bridgewater College in Bridgewater, Virginia. He is the author of *Blacks Run: An American Stream* (Center for American Places, 1999) and a contributing photographer to *The Great Valley Road of Virginia: Shenandoah Landscapes from Prehistory to the Present* (University of Virginia Press, 2010). He is currently working on *Source and Confluence: Exploring the Chesapeake Bay Watershed.*

**Scott Hamilton Suter**, Associate Professor of English and American Studies, lives in Spring Creek, Virginia and teaches literature and American culture courses at Bridgewater College in Bridgewater, Virginia. He has published and lectured on a wide range of topics, including the work of David Lynch, World War I humor, and nineteenth-century pottery traditions, and is the author of *Shenandoah Valley Folklife* (University Press of Mississippi, 1999). Much of his research focuses on the material folk culture of the Shenandoah Valley region. He has enjoyed Shenandoah Valley apples his entire life.

# Acknowledgments

I once asked an apple grower whom he thought I might interview for this project and which types of questions to ask. He replied, "You need to talk to the people who are passionate. You don't even need to ask them; they're going to tell you. It's just gonna flow. You will meet some fine people and make some good friends." Work of this nature depends entirely on the trust and collaboration of others. I would first like to thank the many fine friends who trusted me with their passionate insights and stories for this project, offered me hospitality in their homes, orchards, and workplaces, and provided good company and conversation over coffee and lunch. In particular, Bill Huehn, Peter Cook, Diane Kearns, and Carroll Ryan were instrumental in supporting this project and helping me make contacts with others in the apple industry. To all who participated, this book is your story and I hope I have made you proud.

Faculty research grants from Bridgewater College and Eastern Mennonite University made time and money available to record the photographs and interviews, as did an individual artist grant from the Arts Council of the Valley. A matching grant from the Old Time Apple Growers Association helped immensely at a crucial moment in fundraising for the publication of this book.

**Shenandoah Valley Apples would not have been impossible without the generous support of:**

Eva M. Baez

Esther Bartel and Marilyn and Ray Huss

Richard W. Blizzard

Harry F. Byrd

Elizabeth and John Calabria

Annonymous, The Community Foundation

Peter J. and Elizabeth S. Cook

Ed and Nan Covert

Daniel M. and Mary Jane Davis

Conrad Erb

Terry Evans

Lori and Ken Gano-Overway

Mary L. Greene

Sheila Hagenhofer

Saralyn Reece Hardy

Todd Hedinger and Ann-Janine Morey

Herbert and Irene Holm

Kathleen Holm

Mary Bob Holm

Susan Holm

Jerry L. and Mary L. Holsopple

William G. Huehn

Lora Jost and Chuck Epp

Walter and Mary Ann Jost

Diane Kearns

Geraldine and Bruce Kiefer

Gail Lutsch and Wayne Wiens

Ellen and Larry Martin

Dietrich E. and Audrey J. Maune

Michelle C. McCreery and William Mark Duff

Katerina Moloni and Mark Friesen

Cleveland Morris

Judith Nachison

Kathy O'Hara

Robert W. Regier

Rockbridge Camera Club

Jean G. Roland

Elizabeth M. Seder

Frank Shaw and Mary Kay

Cynthia Smith

Mary Jean Speare and Larry C. Taylor

Mr. and Mrs. Phillip Stone

Kathleen Temple and Ted Grimsrud

Rose M. Volpe

Howard Zehr

Special thanks to George F. Thompson for believing in this project early on, and for gifted insights into sequencing images and text that helped shape the book. Thank you to my friend and colleague Scott Suter for the historical introduction, Brandy Savarese and Kathlene Boone for editing, Stefan Coisson for the visual design, and Stephen DeSantis for finally and capably bringing this book into publication. I have enjoyed working with all of you.

Many people have contributed to my creative well-being and helped me grow personally and professionally over time. I would especially like to thank Saralyn Reece Hardy and Terry Evans for providing opportunities and connections early on, Robert Regier and Howard Zehr for friendship and mentoring, and Bridgewater College art department colleagues Michael Hough, Nan Covert, and Eric Kniss for their support and inspiration.

Finally, I owe my greatest gratitude to my wife Kathy Holm and my children Evan Jost and June Holm. I love you.

Columbia College Chicago Press
600 South Michigan Avenue
Chicago, Illinois 60605-1996, U.S.A.
colum.edu/cccpress


Distributed by the University of Virginia Press
upress.virginia.edu


ISBN: 978-1-935195-46-7